Drew,
What a pleasure it was to meet you! Keep spreading positivity and awareness and self love! With Love + Light,

A SINGLE MOM'S GUIDE TO
RAISING BLACK (GENTLE) MEN

SANYA SIMMONS

TABLE OF CONTENTS

GRATITUDE

My heart is full of wonder and gratitude.

For God's grace that gave me two sons and the strength to raise them into the wonderful human beings they are today.

For my sons Tommy and Matt. They challenge me, inspire me, and bring me great joy. Without their support, this book would not exist.

For my mom, Olivia, my example of what a mother should be. Her support and love through some of my toughest parenting challenges (even when I resisted her help) will never be forgotten.

For my Abuela, Verdelle. Her relationship with my dad and uncle was a role model for what I hoped to achieve with my sons. She also gifted me with my personal copy of *The Prophet*, which means the world to me and is quoted in this book.

For my sisters, Tanya and Kim. I'm truly fortunate to have them by my side walking this road of motherhood with me. They're not only my sisters, but they're also my confidantes and best friends.

For my Daddy, Tommy. He is a good man and a loving father. So much so that I named my firstborn son after him.

For Regina, who has been a safe person with whom I could always share my true feelings.

For Doug, my love, whose love and gentle encouragement helped me to redefine myself and reach for my dreams.

For all my children's uncles, aunts, godparents, and cousins who love them, support us, and pray for us.

For Janet, my first La Leche League Leader. She validated my instincts and introduced me to the concept of mothering through breastfeeding. For my co-Leader and friend, Sandra, whose warmth, empathy, and wisdom know no bounds. For La Leche League International and all the mothers and Leaders who informed and enriched my parenting with their mother-to-mother support.

For Mary Sheedy Kurcinka for her books *Raising Your Spirited Child* and *Kids, Parents, & Power Struggles*. Those books were instrumental in helping this single mom raise an undiagnosed child on the autism spectrum.

For Tempie, who read my first draft of this book and with compassion told me that it wasn't finished...and because she also believed I had something important to say and encouraged me to complete what I had started.

For Mrs. Alice, who still has her copy of my first draft and kept speaking life into my book. She was convinced that I would publish it and told me so every chance she got.

For Carla, whose gift of *The Artist's Way* was perfectly timed and taught me that "Art is not about thinking something up. It is about the opposite – getting something down."

For Heather, for encouraging me and allowing God to use her to let me know that the time is now. And for seeing and supporting my vision of this book and helping me to make it even more personal.

For Marcia, Andrew, Maris, Brandee, Robbie, Kim, Rudy, Warren, Robert, Cindy, Karen, Glenda, and all the teachers and educators, administrators, and coaches who took an interest in my sons and took them under their wings.

For Marcia, Beth-Sarah, Duane, and Veleria for their support and willingness to endorse this first-time author. I'm humbled by their kindness.

For Tesha, for stepping in for me in a big way when I most needed help. For my village, too many to name.

For all the other single moms who are on this journey with me. For my readers. May you find hope within these pages and strength to travel the road that lies ahead.

With love and light,

Sanya

FOREWORD

Being a mother can be one of the most rewarding and difficult jobs. However, it is one that most mothers would not trade for the world. Raising African American boys takes motherhood to another level.

I met Sanya when I taught her oldest son in high school. He is genuinely kind, smart, funny, and handsome. I would later meet her youngest son and he possessed the same traits, but he is very different. The common denominator between the young men is their amazing mother.

When she told me she was writing this book I encouraged her to push forward and share it with the world. I knew she had resources and strategies that could and would help other mothers. When she asked me to write the foreword, I was even more excited because I knew her experiences and support would help other mothers.

This book is destined to be a bestseller as Sanya tells her story from an authentic place. I highly recommend that mothers of African American boys and mothers to be, read this book and utilize the valuable lessons.

Dr. Marcia Gibbs Credle

Motivational Speaker and Author of *Grateful for the Journey*

DEDICATION

To all the brave single moms, I see you.

INTRODUCTION: MAN VS GENTLEMAN

I wasn't always a single mom, nor did I ever intend to be. Yet it is a role that I have owned for almost twenty years. This book is what I searched for when my sons were young but could never find. I wanted practical tips about what to do and how to respond to the multifold challenges I encountered on a daily basis. Skip the theory and the academic philosophies, thank you very much. Just tell me what to do! I was also disheartened to find that most of the books on raising black boys were written by MEN. While their input is extremely important and valid, none of them could tell me what I— as a single woman—should and could do to effectively raise my sons to be the men that I wanted them to become.

I have much respect and appreciation for the vital role that fathers and other important male role models play in the lives of boys. There is absolutely no substitute for a man in a boy's life! Unfortunately, the reality is that many single mothers, including myself, find themselves thrust into the role of being the sole parent in their sons' lives. Rather than accepting defeat in this situation, we can and must do everything within our power to provide a stable environment rich with opportunities for our sons to learn what it means to become men… in spite of and yes, even because of, the absence of their biological fathers.

My ex-husband and I once had a heated discussion about parenting. This was while we were still married. He emphatically told me, "I'M going to make him a man!" My instant reply was, "Yes, you ARE going to make him a man and I'M going to make him a GENTLE man!" My sisters, I tell you that our roles as mothers are no less important than the roles of fathers. We parent differently, yet we have a responsibility to ourselves, to our sons, and to our society, to mother our sons well and to ensure that we prepare them to become all that God has intended for them to be!

This is the story of my parenting journey as the mother of two Black sons. I was contemplating if it'd bother the people—my children and ex-husband—mentioned in this book to be talked about so openly. And at first, I was reluctant to do so, which led me to leave out major insightful details about my journey. You see, my story is their story. One friend told me, *"Your book is good, Sanya, but it's not finished."* Another friend mentioned how much she liked one chapter where I shared a personal story. That's when I knew what I had to do. In order to make this book a resource for moms like me, I had to be open and willing to talk about the real challenges we faced. It was only by giving real-life examples that our story came alive. I'm so grateful to have the full support and permission of both my children—Tommy and Matt. Even my ex-husband gave his consent when I explained to him how I spoke of him within these pages. Their courage and willingness to allow me to tell our story inspires me. I hope you will see that even in the midst of difficult circumstances, love wins.

CHAPTER 1
GET RID OF YOUR ANGER

Okay, I bet it might make you a little angry when I say, 'Get Rid of Your Anger!' What is she talking about? Does she think I can just throw my anger in the trash? How am I supposed to get rid of it? Believe me, I understand. Everything I'm going to say in this book is something I have experienced personally. I'm sharing it here in hopes that it might just help you. Oh, and let's be clear… I'm not talking about the stereotypical "angry black woman" anger. That's not real. I'm talking about the real, and often justifiable, anger. The thing is, if we don't get rid of it, it will inevitably hurt us and our children in the long run. And no mother wants that, right?

Personally, the things that never failed to make me angry were circled around child support and missed visitation. Financial hardship is real and what breaks a single mom's heart is that despite working late shifts and not being able to spend quality time with our babies, we often aren't able to fulfill all their needs. Seeing my children crying because they missed their dad was heartbreaking. Yet calling him repeatedly did not solve the problem. He simply ignored my calls, and I got more and more enraged, but I eventually realized that you can't squeeze blood out of a turnip. Life as a single mother taught me that I had to go with the mindset that I am fully responsible for my kids. Anything that I received from him in terms of money or even "a break" in the form of him taking them for a weekend was a bonus.

Let me give you an example of being prepared for the worst when you are raising your kids alone. As part of my divorce decree, my ex-husband was responsible for our children's health insurance. He was working at a job where he had free benefits, so it literally cost him nothing. However, one day, I received a notice from their pediatrician informing me that there was a bill on their account... because their insurance had denied the claim. I called immediately only to find out that the policy was canceled because their dad had lost the job that covered their insurance. Initially, I was furious! But the good news was that I saw it coming when I took sole responsibility for my children. Therefore, I had already prepared for it, and the boys were covered on my insurance, too.

I'm telling you this story so that you can see how we do play a part in our own situation and our own anger. If I had not prepared for this, my anger would have been not only directed at him but also, at myself. Why? Because, after being with a person for years, you get a better understanding of how they are. So, I knew his track record. Ask yourself this: Are you making decisions and expecting things that are not realistic? This can be a big source of anger. Don't live your life based on what *should* be. You can save yourself so much heartache by planning and living within your own means. Yes, it's hard, but we're stronger than we think. If we put forth the effort, God always provides.

Now, think of one small way that you can get rid of your own anger and resentment about your situation. Remind yourself that it is what it is, and wallowing in self-pity will serve no purpose. Anger is a secondary emotion. It usually stems from a multitude of primary emotions, such as, hurt, betrayal, disappointment, fear, shame, and embarrassment. It is imperative that you resolve all those feelings in order to become an effective parent to your sons. This is not a one-time event, either. You may find yourself experiencing these emotions at pivotal moments in your and your children's lives. Stay in tune with your feelings. And the best way to do that is to revisit this topic often.

Whenever anger rears its ugly head, do some soul search-ing. Journaling is a great way to get your anger out by putting it on paper. When I first started writing this book seven years ago, it was extremely therapeutic for me. I'm a big proponent of finding the "why" in a situation. *Why do I feel this way? Why now? What was the trigger?* Once I have determined the cause, I'm able to resolve the issue for good. This took a lot of work, and a willingness to be honest with myself. I am also lucky to have a couple of trust-worthy friends who are brutally honest with me – even when the truth seems dif-ficult for me to hear.. They are the friends who never judge me and who can be trusted with my innermost secrets. They never use their knowledge of my most personal feelings and experiences against me because they love me unconditionally. Therefore, from my experi-ence, I'd say we all need such a friend. It doesn't have to be a large group; just one or two such friends who understand you are enough. I'd recommend a female friend to avoid the complications, which could arise from close friendships with men.

If you are having trouble letting go of anger or resentment or any other feelings or issues, you may benefit from counseling. Your effectiveness as a mother, as well as your child's emotional health, depends on your mental and spiritual health!

CHAPTER 2
REMEMBER THE GOOD

Remember the good things about his dad... and TELL him about them! Be honest with yourself. Unless your child is the product of violence, you chose to be with his father. What did you like about him? Is he handsome? Charming? Funny? If you can't think of anything good to say, think of his heavenly Father. You might also consider revisiting Chapter One.

Genetics are amazing! As much as I like to think my kids look like me, they do also very much resemble their father. The way they look, stand, walk, talk... at any given moment, I can see their father in them. One of my sons is so much like his dad it's uncanny. It's my youngest one, and he doesn't even remember living with both parents. Yet his personality is the same. Even though it reminds me of his father and not all of my memories with him are pleasant, I've learned to look at him and see the things that I once loved about my ex-husband. He's one of the nicest people you could ever meet. He can talk to anyone and make them feel important, seen, and heard. He's charming and genuinely cares about people.

The harder part for me was to find a way, without being too negative, to help my son to be better than his dad in the things that caused him challenges in life. I had to teach him to be dependable and responsible without focusing on his dad lacking any traits. For example, focusing on my ex-husband's charm, I told my son that charm will only take him so far. He needs to back it up with action and substance. I said that *without* pointing out the negative traits in his dad. Kids are smart. They already know. At other times, I would just say, "You are so much like your dad." When he asked if that's good or bad, I honestly answered, "Both," and laughed. Then we were able to talk about the good things and the challenges with the emphasis on the fact that none of us are perfect. We're all trying to be the best people we can be.

A boy will identify with his father, whether your son talks to you about his dad or not. Make sure he feels comfortable talking to you about him. Whether you intend to or not, failure to speak openly about his dad in a positive way will set up a crisis for your son. He will feel a need to choose sides. You must understand that his love for his father has nothing to do with his love for you. Embrace it... don't ever attempt to compete with it. Even the most irresponsible fathers deserve to be treated with respect. Children are very observant. They don't need their mothers to tell them what their father did or did not do for them. They already know. A loving mother will always do what is best for her child, including only speaking about his father in the most positive light possible.

My children missed their father dearly while they were growing up. We were married for nine and a half years. He even cut both their umbilical cords. Yet after our divorce, he was mostly absent in their lives during their formative years. I didn't speak to our sons about his shortcomings. I simply told them that I knew their father loves them, which I absolutely knew to be true. I told them that whatever it was that was keeping him away from them must be pretty bad, because he would never want to miss out on being with them, and that we needed to pray for him. Not only did this help them, but it also helped me to remember that he was doing the best he could with what he had to work with. I know that I made the right decision to divorce him, yet I never disrespected him as their father. I will always be grateful to him for giving me two wonderful sons.

The good news is that I was right! Our grown children now have a good relationship with their father. They communicate with him regularly and see him several times a year. He sends birthday and Christmas gifts. They were groomsmen at his wedding. They go to family reunions, and spend occasional holidays with their dad. I never would have imagined these possibilities when we were going through the worst times, but I'm so glad I left the door open for them to have this relationship, no matter how long it took to get to this point. Seeing them happy is all I ever wanted.

CHAPTER 3
MAKE SURE HE KNOWS THAT HE IS LOVED

A mother's first and most important job is to pour love into her children. Everything else flows from there. It's the one thing that can't be faked or replaced. Take every opportunity to speak life into him. Point out his strengths and help him to build on those strengths. Tell him what positive qualities you see in him, so that he will have a healthy self-esteem. There are so many obstacles that we, as humans, face every day at work, school, and even among "friends." Your son will inevitably deal with criticism and negativity outside your home. Society often works to diminish a young man's spirit, especially a young Black man who is full of energy. Home should be a safe haven where your son feels free to be himself and is loved unconditionally.

Speaking from my personal experience, I had set some ground rules regarding what was acceptable and what wasn't in our house. I had no tolerance for words or actions that would bring someone down or hurt one's self esteem. For example, my kids were not allowed to say *"I hate you"* to each other. I always corrected them saying, *"No, you don't. You might be angry, but you don't hate your brother.*

11

Your brother should be your best friend. He's the one who will always be there for you. Don't say things that hurt. Don't hit below the belt. Love each other. When I'm gone from this earth, you will always have each other."

I know this probably sounds simplistic, but it really works! My kids are completely different from one another in terms of their interests and peer groups. However, I find it fascinating how they put their differences aside and always find a way to spend time with each other. They share a bond that is independent of their relationship with me. I often hear them up late at night talking and laughing and watching shows together, and it warms my heart. We have created this bond within our home that allows each of them to feel loved and important. That gives them strength and confidence to stand tall in the face of adversity and to truly go after their dreams.

Let me give you another example. My oldest son is on the autism spectrum. When he was younger, he used to say terrible, mean things to his baby brother. It was a struggle for me as their mother! If you know anyone on the autism spectrum, you have probably experienced their "commitment" to what they think is right. (I put that in quotes, because it's a nice way of saying good luck getting them to change their behavior!) See how I chose a word that is seen as more positive? Every trait they have can be seen in a positive light. It's our job as mothers to teach them to use their character traits to their benefit instead of hurting themselves or others.

So, what did I do about him verbally abusing his brother? I turned it upside down! I told my youngest son not to worry about it. I said, *"That's just Tommy language for 'I love you!'"* It worked! In doing that, I helped Matt to better understand his brother, and refused to let his brother's shortcomings affect him in a hurtful way. I promise you I was just trying to get through each moment, showing love to both kids. I didn't see the long-term benefits that would come from such creative parenting on my part. Now, I'm amazed at how compassionate and understanding Matt is with anyone he meets who might also be on the spectrum or facing some other hardship or emotional or mental challenge.

Kids sometimes take a mother's love for granted. They might think we're just saying those things because we have to. They think we're biased. Sometimes, we are, but that's okay! Keep speaking truth, life, and love into your son anyway! You'll also want to surround him with other people who love him and will stand in for you when you're not around. Our support system, our "village" comes in to fill in the gaps. Relatives, neighbors, coaches, church family, his friends' moms. Remember you're not alone, and you're not helpless. Reach out and ask for help and support when you need it!

It's also important to tell your son that his father loves him, even if he is absent from his life. As I mentioned before, I always told my kids that I knew their father loved them. I didn't make excuses for him. I said I didn't understand what was keeping him from them, but I knew he loved them. Share memories and pictures, if you have them. He needs to know that regardless of what the situation is right now, there is a seed of love that can be nurtured when the time is right. If that's not something he will believe, because of his own personal experience, tell him that God loves him! Every child is a gift from God, and he needs to know that he is NOT a mistake!

CHAPTER 4
EVERYONE HAS A GIFT

Everyone has a gift and a purpose in life! Help your son to find his. Encourage him and provide him with opportunities to explore and develop his gifts. Appreciate and applaud his accomplishments... be his biggest advocate! He may be good at many things. Don't let him fall into the trap of being a jack of all trades and master of none. It is great to be well-rounded and to have options. Some talents may combine well for unique vocations. The key is to focus on which God-given gift makes him extraordinary- what is his true calling, something that comes naturally to him, and that he does far better than any of his peers, or perhaps anyone you know. It's important to emphasize and enhance his natural abilities and talents because many people can study hard and get good grades. On the contrary, many intellectually gifted people do not get good grades, but they excel in their respective profession. If you focus on the gift and not the labels, you will be able to help your son find his purpose in life.

Help your son to find his own way. He may be a football player, or a pianist. He may like theater or soccer instead. Does he love to read or draw... or would he rather take things apart and put them back together? Focus on his interests rather than forcing him to be what you (or society) think(s) he should be!

Once you have helped him to identify his gifts, genuinely support his dreams while also offering options he may not see for himself. Is a four-year college the best way to achieve his goals or would a trade school be better suited to meet his needs? Share your experience to help him explore his options but don't think that your life experience will always be best for him. Encourage him to dream… and teach him how to bring his dreams to life.

My son Matt is a dreamer. He often says things like, *"I need 100k by the end of this year."* This frustrates me to no end, and I used to tell him that he was talking nonsense! I wouldn't listen to him because it sounded unreasonable to me… and I worried that the only way he could get 100k would be by doing something illegal. He misinterpreted my frustration and felt that I was not being supportive of him. I love him too much for something like this to come between us. It was hard, but I finally figured out a way to have an honest conversation with him. I talked to him about my fears and explained that I have complete faith in him. I believe he can do anything he sets his mind to… and works for. Pie in the sky dreams do not replace hard work and planning.

We talked about the fact that there are some people who are free spirits and prefer entrepreneurial work. They make their own way. Others prefer the stability of traditional jobs with benefits and regular paychecks. I happen to prefer stability over risk. However, my son is someone who thinks everything through and takes calculated risks. There is value to both perspectives. True success and happiness lie somewhere in-between the two. This understanding and mutual respect is key to any discussion. I explained that in order for me to support him, and for him to achieve his goals, he has to have a specific plan to make it happen. I also gave examples of other people in our family who share his entrepreneurial spirit and might be able to help him in ways that are more difficult for me to understand. The cool thing is that in acknowledging my challenges with taking calculated risks, I realized how I've been holding myself back just because I was afraid of taking risks. This conversation with my son helped me make creative leaps in my own life—like the one I'm taking in publishing this book!

It's important to share your process and how you approach business and career decisions with your son. It's really never too soon to start. Whether he is deciding what classes to take in school or what extra-curricular activities to pursue, or deciding what internship to take, teach him how to plan for his own future based on his own dreams and aspirations. This will give him the confidence to be able to make such decisions, while knowing that you will have his back. Be the example for him to follow. He'll believe what he sees more than what he hears. Seeing you discover and embrace your own gifts will show him that he can do the same with his. Share your planning and milestones with him. He will start to use those steps and strategies in his own life as well as value your advice even more. As he becomes an adult, you can challenge, encourage, and even push each other to greater heights. That's when things really start to get fun!

CHAPTER 5
DON'T IGNORE BAD BEHAVIOR

Okay, now that we've talked about all the feel-good stuff, it's time to deal with the hard stuff, too. Yes, every child has a gift. Every child also has a unique set of challenges. As moms, we want to protect our children. The best way to do that is to be honest with ourselves about both their gifts and their challenges.

Don't ignore his bad behavior. You know your son! Be honest with yourself and with him. Address the behavior, and help him to understand that he is a good person who sometimes makes bad or inappropriate choices. I can't stress enough about separating the person from the behavior. If you want to raise a young man to be a gentleman, you have to help him see himself as a good person. Then help him identify and change the behaviors that don't go along with the type of man he wants to be.

My oldest son, Tommy, was hurting his little brother. He was also strangling stuffed animals. Many years later, he told me that he was simply acting out something he had seen on tv. Back then, it was alarming, to say the least. He also got in trouble in school when another child said he wanted to kill himself, and Tommy suggested a way of doing it. He was eight years old. At the same time, I could not get him to sleep at night. It was a vicious cycle of long days, tantrums, and sleepless nights. I was at my wit's end. I could also see a look in his eyes that just "wasn't right." We had always been very close, and suddenly I wasn't able to reach him emotionally anymore. At least, I didn't feel like I was reaching him in a way that was making a difference in his behavior. I do believe that our children hear us, even when they're unable to respond. It's like putting money in the bank and the bank puts a hold on the money. It was there, but I couldn't access it at the time.

In the meantime, I needed IMMEDIATE help. One night, it got so bad that I took him to the emergency room. That was the first time anyone outside the family told me that he might have a high-functioning form of autism. (My sister, who is a trained professional, had tried to tell me, but I wasn't ready to hear it.) He was only eight years old. Looking back, I had always instinctively known how to manage his triggers and redirect his behavior. We have to know when we have reached our limit and when it's time to reach out for professional help. The diagnosis felt right to me because I looked at his behaviors candidly and realized that he absolutely exhibited all the signs. Know when you need help, and reach out as soon as possible. Don't let pride get in the way. That's the only way to solve problems before they escalate.

Being honest with yourself about your son's behavior can also help you avoid misdiagnoses. There had been teachers who tried to label Tommy "emotional/behavioral disordered" and "Attention Deficit/Hyperactivity Disorder" (ADHD). This is very common among black boys in schools. Teachers and administrators rush to judge or label them without truly seeing them for who they are. It is a struggle we—as moms of Black boys—must be aware of so that we can arm ourselves with knowledge. Know which battles to fight.

On the other hand, there are inevitably going to be times when your child is in the wrong. No child is perfect. That's when it's very important to teach him how to own up to his mistakes and to instill trust in him and in those who are working with him. I have one big rule with my sons; we can get through anything together. I will always help you, as long as you tell me the truth.

Matt once got into serious trouble in high school, along with some of his friends. He was not a major offender, but he was present and participated in the events that happened. He is adamant about not "snitching" on his friends. When Matt was interviewed by the administrators and the school police, he admitted what he had done and took responsibility for his part in the situation. He also said what he didn't do and defended himself where it was necessary to do so, and his story was proven to be true. They believed him. He was suspended, pending a hearing before the disciplinary panel at the district level. I was there with him for the hearing. The school officer actually spoke on his behalf, as did the assistant principal. This is something they had told me they would not do. They advocated for him to be allowed back in school instead of sending him to an alternative school. When I had a chance to speak, I told the panel that I have taught my son to always tell the truth… and if he told the truth he would be better off than if he lied. I appealed to them as a mom. I asked them to please help me by showing him that I was right… that because he had proven himself trustworthy, he was worth making an exception and allowing him to return to school. I didn't make excuses for him. I acknowledged his behavior, made him own up to it and showed him how to earn back trust when it had been broken. The panel chose to allow him to return to school. Every other student who was involved in that incident was sent to the alternative school. There were stipulations. He had to sign a behavior contract, and I was supportive of that. The point for me was not to pretend it didn't happen. He needed consequences, but we were able to mitigate those consequences with subsequent good behavior.

If you address bad behavior when it happens, those can be pivotal points in a young man's development. It isn't easy. The good news is that by dealing with the difficult stuff now, you avoid a lot of heartache in the future. You're also building a bond with your son that can never be broken. He'll know he can reach the stars when his mom has his back through good times and bad because he'll know that he is loved for who he truly is and not who you want him to be. The irony is that in doing so, you'll help shape him into the kind of person you hope he will be!

CHAPTER 6
LOOK FOR THE "WHY" BEHIND THE BEHAVIOR

Acknowledging bad behavior isn't enough. You also need to look for the "why" behind the behavior and give him an opportunity to speak. If you don't teach him cause and effect and how to more effectively solve his problems at home, he'll learn it the hard way in the streets. Effectively means maintaining control of himself so as never to allow himself to fall subject to negative stereotypes. Teach him to always present himself the way he wants to be perceived. Don't let the "why" be an excuse. Once you understand it, you can come up with a strategy to overcome it.

I know, I said I'm writing this book to give practical strategies and not a lot of theoretical rambling. You want examples, right? Okay, here we go. Think about the things your son does that absolutely drive you crazy. Does it take forever for you to get him to put on socks? Does he complain about how the socks bother him when he puts on his shoes? How about tags in his shirts? Does he say they're itchy? Maybe he HATES the blanket you bought to replace his old worn out one? These are all signs that he probably has sensory issues. He's not trying to be difficult. These things really do cause him distress. If you acknowledge this and honor what he is trying to tell you, it becomes much easier to help him find a better way to express himself.

This is not an excuse to have a tantrum. Don't expect him to know how to express himself at first. Teach him to use his words to tell you what's bothering him. It takes time. You might have to give him the words. For instance, if you see him bothered and unable to express himself, you might say, "I see you scratching. Is that tag in your shirt bothering you? Let's cut it off. Would you like to try some shirts that don't have tags in them? Let me help you adjust those socks so they don't bother your feet. Do you think you can get through today with these, please? I know they don't feel good. I just don't have any other socks for you to wear today. They also make socks without seams. I'll make sure I buy those for you the next time we go shopping, okay?"

Some moms believe in a "tough love" approach to parenting. They're afraid of being too soft, or they act out of frustration when faced with a child's emotions and negative behavior. They tell their children, "Get over it. Toughen up. It's not that bad." This can be very damaging to a child's self-esteem. Your son's feelings are real. I'm not saying that his feelings justify bad behavior. I'm saying respect, acknowledge, and empathize with his feelings. By doing this, you put yourself on your child's team. Now, you can work together to find a solution!

Sometimes, as moms, we have to plan better for success. My son, Tommy, used to have meltdowns when we were out running errands all day. I had a to-do list that I was determined to accomplish, and I got so frustrated. I would have a meltdown, too! Many of our activities were centered around a mother-to-mother support group I was leading, and there were lots of other children around for hours. It could be noisy and overstimulating for him. At this point, I didn't know he was on the autism spectrum. I just knew that he had a threshold and could only tolerate so much before his behavior spiraled out of control. He would hit or refuse to share toys or cry or become very clingy… or all of the above. I learned that our outings could be more successful if I made sure he was well-rested and had a quiet morning before taking him into a high-stimulus environment. I also learned that sometimes, I needed to leave a situation when I saw his anxiety level rising. This was MY responsibility as his mother to know his limits and to set him up for success. Sometimes, this meant my to-do list didn't get finished. It was much better to go home with both of us happy and smiling than to force a situation and then blame him for not knowing how to handle the stress I had imposed on him.

This also taught me to respect my own limitations. When I take care of myself as a mother and my needs for rest, food, quiet time, and allow myself opportunities to recharge my batteries, I am better equipped to be the loving mother I want to be. By setting this example for him, I taught Tommy to manage his own sensory and physical triggers. It's amazing to me how well he has carried those lessons with him into adulthood. He is doing a fantastic job as an adult. He even told me recently that he was uncomfortable at a new job, but he knew he had to be friendly, so he was exhausted when he got home. He said it took about two weeks for him to adjust. I can't even begin to express how much it warmed my heart to hear him verbalize the coping skills I began teaching him when he was just a toddler!

Remember that focusing on the "why" behind the behavior is not about making excuses for it. It's also not resigning yourself to being defeated. It's about teaching your son to take responsibility for himself and his life and showing him that he CAN WIN in SPITE of his challenges… and even be BETTER BECAUSE of them!!!

CHAPTER 7
LET HIM
EXPERIENCE FAILURE

Let him experience failure while he's still at home with you. That way, you'll be there to pick him up and teach him how to pick himself up, find another strategy, and try again. I believe that young men need to experience failure and learn to solve problems on their own. Home should be a safe place for your son to learn these critical life skills.

I know this might sound crazy, but hear me out. No mother wants to see her child fail. Their failure actually feels like our failure. If only we were better mothers, our kids would be successful. Right? Wrong. No matter how well we parent, there are no guarantees in life. Our job is to teach them how to overcome challenges and how to persevere. It's also extremely important to teach them to learn from their mistakes. I believe we repeat our mistakes until we learn the lesson behind them. I try my best to learn the lesson the first time!

Here's an example. Tommy's first job was in a fast-food restaurant. Remember that he is on the autism spectrum, and one of the effects of his autism is not always responding appropriately in social situations. One day, he was at work when a co-worker made an inappropriate sexual comment to him. It was conversational and not directed at him specifically, but he responded with what he thought was a joke. That person, who was male, then accused Tommy of sexually harassing him... because Tommy is gay. It didn't matter that many other employees frequently made inappropriate comments in this work environment. It only mattered that this guy accused my son of sexual harassment. He was terminated.

I was FURIOUS! I wanted to sue the company for discrimination based on his sexual orientation. I wanted to meet with the General Manager and the Human Resources Department at the franchise level. I was determined to get his job back, but the reality is he didn't need to work there anyway. He insisted that I back down and let it go. It was so hard for me to do that. I was worried that he wouldn't be able to find another job after being fired, especially since he was terminated for sexual harassment. I was embarrassed by his behavior because I was a former restaurant General Manager. Surely, my child should know better. I felt like his behavior was a reflection of my parenting. It wasn't.

Instead of trying to fix a toxic situation, I talked to Tommy about learning the lesson. I made sure he understood why he had lost his job, and what his part in the situation was. He couldn't control what the other person had said, but he could certainly control how he responded. This was not easy to get through to him, because fairness is VERY important to him. It's part of his autism. Things need to make sense to him logically, and this didn't. We worked through it, though, and he found another job without my help. In spite of my fears, he has been a very successful employee ever since, even holding multiple jobs at once. He learned a valuable lesson through that experience that he might not have learned if he did not have the chance to fail.

Along with failure comes mistakes. He needs to learn the art of sincere apology. Never make him say he's "sorry" when he's not. When he does apologize, he needs to be able to tell you specifically what he's apologizing for and how he intends to make it right. Make him focus on his part. His first attempts may be awkward and clumsy, but that's okay. That's how he learns. He will develop his own style that works for him. A great place to practice is with his siblings. You have an awesome opportunity as a mom to show (and tell) how each person played a part in their arguments. For example, both of my sons love to pick at each other and push each other's buttons. When the other one has had enough, the fights can be huge... even the play fights! It's not helpful to pick sides. Have you ever told an older sibling not to hit their younger sibling? Did you also correct the younger sibling for picking the fight in the first place? By making each person take responsibility for his own actions, you help to strengthen their relationship and avoid causing resentments that could last a lifetime.

Another example of a situation that can be used as a learning experience is when they get a bad grade in school or perhaps a poor progress report. When they were young, I did help facilitate conversations with their teachers... but I gradually gave more and more of the responsibility to them. By the time they were in high school, I insisted that they meet with their teachers and "come up with a plan." I was happy to talk them through what they might say if they wanted help before going to talk to the teacher. Then I also assured them that I believed in them and their ability to solve the problem. Words are important. By acknowledging that there was a problem and showing confidence in their ability to solve their own problems, I was preparing them to solve their own problems in life. Following up with them after the fact is important too. Believe me, they didn't always have those conversations immediately no matter how many times I said it or encouraged them to do it. Sometimes they flat out failed to do it. In that case, I allowed them to fail. There's value in that lesson too.

Tommy always waited until the last minute to finish assignments. He only did what he felt like doing, and no one (not even I) could make him do anything he thought was stupid. Whether that was an essay or studying for a test, it didn't matter. His senior year in high school was extremely stressful for me. He wasn't bothered at all. I was determined that he would get all his work done and pass the necessary classes, including extra classes he had to take online. The administration worked with us to develop a plan to help him, but he had to do the work. He didn't even attempt the online courses. One day, we were in the school counselor's office for a meeting about his graduation requirements, and she told me, "It might not be a bad thing if he stays another year." That was the first time I even considered that as an option. It was like a weight was taken off my shoulders. He didn't seem to mind at all. He watched his classmates graduate without him and stayed for the fifth year in high school. He made the best of it, and he even chose to stay the entire year instead of one semester. He took one required class in the fall and one in the spring. He filled the rest of his schedule with the Fine Arts classes that he loved, and he truly had an enjoyable, stress-free year. The extra time also allowed him to mature a bit. He later told me that he endured some awful teasing from the other students who knew he should have graduated the year before and that he learned from that experience. Another consequence was that he had already "maxed out" his eligibility in the Marching Band, so he had to miss out on his absolute favorite class.

Whatever the situation may be, don't allow your son to make excuses. Failure can feel like the end of the world for you and him, but most times it's not. Many things will happen that are unfair. Many will happen that are actually a direct result of choices he has made. In either case, he can only control his part. There is power in understanding that!

CHAPTER 8
DON'T LET HIM BE A
"YES" MAN

You also don't want him to be a "yes" man. Give him the gift of discernment. Teach him to respectfully question authority and to make his own decisions. This must include the right to say no to you. I believe that teaching children never to question authority puts them at risk of falling victim to predatory adults. You are your son's first authority figure, so it's important for him to practice with you.

I know this may be different from the way you were raised. I'm not advocating permissive parenting. What I'm saying is that children are people, too. They have their own thoughts, opinions, likes, and dislikes. Choose your battles. Of course, there will be times when you need to stick to your decisions and make sure to hold your son accountable. The key is for you to take your ego out of the equation and not get into power struggles with him. If he doesn't want to drink his milk and wants juice instead, listen to him. I'm not saying you should let him have juice all day. Let him know he can have juice a certain number of times a day. That's your decision in his best interest. Then, he can choose whether to have them all in the morning… or to spread them out throughout the day. Once he has had his allotted number of cups of juice, give him a choice of what he can drink instead. Milk or water, for example. That way, he still has the ability to choose what he wants… from the options you gave him. Other things might be really important to him, but in the grand scheme of things, they aren't that important. Who cares if his clothes don't match? Let him express himself the way he wants.

Some things are important socially, yet no matter how many times you tell him, he still doesn't want to do those. This is where you have to let go and let him learn the lesson. Tommy hated taking showers. Every day was a battle to get him to take one… even after long hours at band camp outside in the heat. I bought deodorant and reminded him every day to wear it, but I wasn't going to physically put it on him. It was up to him. He often smelled like onions or worse, but he didn't care. One day, he "magically" started taking showers. Years later, he admitted to me that a school counselor had called him into the office to tell him that other students were complaining about his body odor. He explained to Tommy how that was having a negative impact on his relationship with his peers. To this day, Tommy never leaves the house without taking a shower first… and most times he wears deodorant too!

Speaking of showers. Have you ever heard the saying *"He must be smelling himself?"* I don't have proof of this other than my experience with my two sons. I think it's a part of their transition to manhood. They seem to LIKE smelling their own body odor because it makes them feel like a man! Don't worry. Keep teaching him about personal hygiene, and this phase will pass.

Another issue in our house is the trash. I'm constantly reminding them to take out the trash. I know it's sexist, but I feel that with two sons in the house, I should never have to do it. That's their job. They always wait until they are almost late for work to leave the house. When I say, "Take out the trash," they sometimes tell me no. It's infuriating. I've learned to allow them to say no, as long as they commit to taking it out as soon as they get home. By doing this, I respect their needs while still holding them accountable for their responsibilities around the house.

Let's talk about hair. Matthew LOVES his long hair! He refuses to cut it low, but he always keeps a fresh fade. When he gets it braided, it really looks nice, but many times it just looks a mess to me. I ask him repeatedly to cut it, but he won't. When he was younger, I probably could have forced him to do it, but I never did. That's a part of who he is and how he sees himself, and I don't have the right to impose my wishes on him. Instead, I talk to him about grooming his hair and help him find products to keep it moisturized and healthy. As he has grown, I have bought products for him to try and then given him the responsibility of replenishing his supply. That's something that goes along with having long hair. Tommy, on the other hand, won't even get an edge up or a fresh shave. He doesn't even brush his hair or his beard most days. While I wish he would pay more attention to his grooming, it's ultimately up to him. I can advise them and give suggestions, but they have the right to say, "No."

As they've gotten older, I can see them taking responsibility for themselves and making decisions that are in their own best interest. Tommy is a hard worker. He used to get called into work almost every time he had a day off. He was exhausted, because he always said, "Yes," when they called. Admittedly, it was also because he loved the money he was making! He eventually got tired of being the only person they called to cover extra shifts. He told his manager that he was no longer willing to be the "go-to" person, giving up all of his days off. He was able to work out a schedule with his manager that worked for both of them. His ability to negotiate his schedule was a direct result of the lessons he learned at home. Tommy tried repeatedly to get Matt to work in the restaurant business with him. Matt was very clear that the restaurant business didn't interest him. He refused to go along the easy path of just accepting that as his only option. He decided the type of work he was willing to do, went after it, and got the job he really wanted. Seeing him making decisions for himself, planning, and succeeding in what he sets out to do is gratifying. I'm extremely proud of both of them.

Parenting this way is not easy! In fact, it takes a lot more work to raise a child to think for himself than it does to be an authoritarian parent. There were so many times I felt frustrated and even angry, questioning myself and my parenting choices. Many people have opinions and like to tell you that you're doing it wrong, too. "That boy is spoiled. You let him run all over you. He needs some discipline!" they will say. It will feel like they're right. You will often be exhausted and unsure of yourself. Remember that the key is for you to make CONSCIOUS choices to allow him to speak his mind and make decisions for himself. It's not giving in to him. It's empowering him and nurturing his confidence and his ability to think and speak up for himself. It's hard work! Do it anyway. Make the investment in your son and the man he will become. He's worth it!

CHAPTER 9
TELL HIM THE TRUTH—
TWO STRIKES

Tell him the truth. He already has two strikes. I love sports analogies. Let's look at this in terms of baseball. He has two strikes against him – he's Black and he's male. One more strike, and he's out. He won't get the benefit of the doubt or second chances in life. Now teach him to work within the system by knowing the rules... and following them... better than anyone else!

My sons get angry with me literally every time I say this to them. They accuse me of exaggerating. They tell me that it's not really as bad as it "used to be." In their minds and in their protected view of the world, I'm overreacting and worrying unnecessarily. This worries me even more. It feels like a double-edged sword because I have intentionally protected them from negative influences and environments as much as I possibly could . My goal was to educate them about the "real" world while also doing my absolute best to keep them safe.

Unfortunately, some lessons are best learned through experience. As many times as we talked about *"driving while Black,"* both of my sons have had more than their share of traffic tickets. Each time, they were at fault. The anxiety and relief I felt were indescribable whenever they walked away from these situations without incident. The reality is that the odds are not in their favor. Something was bound to happen eventually.

Matt was 19 years old when that "something" happened. He was driving alone late at night, speeding through a known speed trap. He got stopped for speeding, and the police officer said he smelled marijuana. There was marijuana in the car, but it wasn't visible. It was inside a closed backpack on the floor behind the passenger seat. Matt was cooperative and gave no reason for the cop to make him get out of the car, but he did. He also proceeded to search the car without Matt's consent. In fact, Matt asked him if he needed a warrant to search, and the officer told him that he knew what he could and couldn't do and proceeded to search without exigent circumstances or a warrant. He ended up getting arrested that night. Remember that I said he was at fault. I'm not making excuses for his poor choices. What I am saying is that there were several instances where if he hadn't been a Black male, he might have ended up with a simple warning rather than being arrested. He might not have been stopped for speeding. He probably would not have been asked to step out of the car. He probably would not have had his rights violated with an illegal search. At the very least, the officer may have listened to him when he asked if he needed a warrant... and called for the warrant before searching the car.

Back to my sports analogies. There is another sport that uses strikes. We're a bowling family, so I much prefer bowling strikes over those in baseball. Not only do you get ten points for each strike, but you also get to rack up extra points from the next two frames. What if we also teach our sons that they have two strikes in their favor? Guess what? Those can be the same two strikes... they're Black and they're male! We can teach them to be proud of who they are BECAUSE they are Black, not in spite of it. I mentioned in previous chapters how important it is to speak life into our sons. When they grow up feeling good about who they are, they stand taller and speak with confidence. It may seem counter-intuitive, but they're also more humble human beings. That's because they don't have anything to prove. They know how to protect themselves without the excessive anger that could put them in harm's way.

Matt was angry and nervous when he got arrested. Yet something in his demeanor must have been cooperative and respectful enough for that officer to treat him with some degree of compassion. He allowed Matt to call a friend to come pick up the car instead of having it impounded. That friend called me, and I was able to go find him and get him out of jail that night. He carried himself with dignity throughout the entire ordeal and came through it ALIVE. He also earned the trust of his lawyer, and that lawyer worked extremely hard on Matthew's behalf and got him a great deal which helped in keeping his record clean. When he went to court, the judge was hard on him, and he respectfully listened to everything she had to say. She signed off on the deal, largely due to the fact that he showed her respect as well as because she could see that he was polite and willing to accept responsibility for his actions.

Even in this difficult situation, it was very important for me to stick to the principles that had been guiding me throughout Matt's childhood. My first priority was to get him out of jail that night. I thought long and hard over whether or not it was the right thing to do. I decided it was. I had always promised him that we could get through anything, as long as he told me the truth. This was the biggest test we had ever had of my unconditional love for him. I wasn't going to let him down when he needed me the most. I even called his dad and gave him a chance to help. He immediately sent money for Matt's bail that same night.

Matt and I didn't talk much that night except for me telling him that I loved him no matter what... and that we would talk about it after we both got some rest. When we did talk, he told me the truth. I told him that the reason I bailed him out was because of my promise of unconditional love. I also let him know that if he ever got arrested again, I would not bail him out. I told him that I would always love him, and I would visit him, but that was a one-time pass.

That situation also gave Matt the opportunity to stand up and accept financial responsibility for his mistake. Without me prompting him to do so, he informed me that he would pay his lawyer and probation fees, and he did. It wasn't easy. It was painful to watch his emotional turmoil as he went through this, but it was an invaluable lesson about how a man takes responsibility for himself and his choices, and learns from the consequences of his actions. I think this is a great example of how the two bowling strikes can outweigh the two baseball strikes if we as mothers will commit to teaching the lessons and then getting out of the way when they have the chance to experience those lessons in real-life situations.

Your son is bound to make mistakes. He isn't perfect. Always remember that his choices and mistakes don't invalidate all the hard work you put into parenting him. Hopefully, you will see maturity, responsibility, and the ability to navigate difficult situations when they arise. That in itself can be very gratifying. It's a sign that your son is becoming a man, perhaps even a gentleman.

CHAPTER 10
KNOW HIS TEACHERS

Know his teachers and administrators, and make them your (and his) allies. Also, know his rights within the educational system.

It is a fact that Black boys are more often diagnosed with ADD/ADHD and behavior disorders than any other demographic group. Know your child and ask questions before just accepting any labels. It is your job and your responsibility to be an active member of your son's student support team. Even the best teachers, doctors, psychologists, and administrators make mistakes. Your input and perspective are critical for a proper diagnosis and setting up the most appropriate education plan for your son.

Tommy showed signs that I saw as gifted behaviors at a very early age. He loved math! He was only five years old when he began drawing huge math charts on the pavement with sidewalk chalk. 1+99=100; 2+98=100... Then, he "leveled up" to higher numbers. 101+99=200; ... 201+199=400... It was impressive! There were other signs, too. When he was in first grade, I asked his teacher to test him for the gifted program. She said, *"I don't think so. I wouldn't recommend testing for that,"* implying that she would test him for a behavioral problem instead. I knew that I had the right to insist on him being tested, so I told her to test him anyway. He tested into the program based on mental ability and academic achievement alone. Which meant that his IQ and standardized test scores were extremely high. His creativity? Not so much. His motivation? Next to nothing. Looking back, I know that we were both right. He was very intellectually gifted, but there was something else going on with him, too.

It wasn't until Tommy was in the third grade that things escalated to the point where I needed help. That was when we found out that he had Asperger's Syndrome, a high-functioning form of autism. The Asperger's diagnosis has since been removed from the Diagnostic and Statistical Manual (DSM) used by psychiatrists to diagnose psychiatric conditions, but I believe it perfectly describes my son.

Those were some extremely challenging years. That's actually an understatement. He had teachers who got into power struggles with him over insignificant things like his habit of tapping his pencil on the desk. This is just a form of self-stimulation (stimming) that is common among people with autism. He was still receiving gifted services one day a week. To receive those services, he had to take a bus to a different school. This was not an ideal situation, because his behavior plan was not properly communicated to the other school's administration. Even though I was in contact with his gifted teacher, she got frustrated with him one day and sent him to the office. Well, Tommy also puts things in his mouth as a form of stimming. He saw a bowl of candy on the principal's desk and took a piece. That principal called the police on him for stealing! This is another example of the baseball two strikes rule. I was mortified when I received a call at work from the police telling me that I needed to pick Tommy up from school, or they would have to take him to juvenile detention. He was eight, and all he had done was tap his pencil on the desk and take a piece of candy to calm his nerves when he was upset.

I wrote a letter to the School Board, but they did nothing. They actually wrote a letter excusing the principal's behavior. At the same time, the District School Psychologist finished her evaluation of Tommy. Even though he had three doctors saying that he had Asperger's, this woman wrote a thirty-page report explaining that he was too verbal to be autistic. He was just "extremely bright, extremely manipulative, and oppositional/defiant." Two strikes again. The sad thing is that this woman's report prevented Tommy from getting the educational diagnosis necessary for him to receive services that would have helped him to be successful in school.

Knowing your child's teachers and administration also means knowing when he is not in an environment where he will be supported, no matter what you do to help him. I made the decision to move to a different school district so he could get the help he needed. The new school district saw that there was a problem and agreed with the diagnosis, although the testing criteria really was not designed to catch someone as high-functioning as Tommy already was. The irony of this still baffles me because he was very verbal and high-functioning as a direct result of all the hard work I had put in with him at home. Thankfully, the new school district found a way to help him anyway. He did exhibit signs of ADHD as a part of his autism, so they used the ADHD diagnosis to offer him special education services. It wasn't until years later, when he was in tenth grade, that we finally got his proper educational diagnosis under the autism spectrum.

I share this story with you because I want you to trust your instincts and be an advocate for your son. Do your best to work with the teachers and administrators. When that's not possible, be prepared to fight for his rights. Also, continue to speak love and life into him. He will need the confidence you instill in him at home as he deals with the system that was not designed to help him. He'll also learn vital lessons from you about how to stand up for himself throughout his life.

I cannot write this chapter without also acknowledging the MANY teachers, school counselors, coaches, and principals who loved my sons. They saw the best in my sons and helped to shape them into the men they are today. The counselor in Tommy's new school district was instrumental in getting him the services he needed when I was at a loss for what to do. Tommy's first case manager in high school did a phenomenal job connecting with him and helping him acclimate to high school. He also had a wonderful relationship with his band director. Matthew really loved his middle school counselor. She saw something in him and knew he could use some encouragement, so she invited him to her "lunch bunch" once a week. That relationship helped him through some very tough times. I often called or emailed the school counselors when I felt they needed emotional support from a licensed professional. One example is when my mom died. I was grieving her death myself, and I knew that they needed more grief support than I was able to give at that time.

Be visible at your son's school. They need to see you as an involved mother. That goes a long way toward him being treated fairly and with care and compassion. Teachers will often go the extra mile for students whose parents are involved in their education. Go to all school orientations. Volunteer to help out with his activities. Be the team mom or sign up to work the band concession stand or as a parent chaperone. That communication is essential between home and school. You know which teachers are your child's advocates. Let them know how much you appreciate them.

When in doubt, ask for help or ask for resources! Schools are required to provide you with the information you need, but they won't know you need it if you don't ask. The laws are constantly changing. Do you know the difference between a 504 Plan and an IEP (Individualized Education Plan)? One is based on the Americans with Disabilities Act (ADA) and the other is based on the Individuals with Disabilities in Education Act (IDEA). Each provides legal protections and accommodations for students. It's your job as the parent to understand these rights so that you can advocate for your son and teach him to advocate for himself. Tommy had an IEP. Matt has Narcolepsy, which is a medical condition that makes it difficult for him to stay awake and interferes with learning. He had a 504 Plan. Both Tommy and Matt had accommodations, including testing accommodations. Things like extra time and scheduled breaks can make a world of difference in leveling the playing field and helping a student to achieve at his highest potential.

I talked to them about their rights and their IEP and 504 Plan so that they also understood what they were able to request from their teachers. I also made sure they participated in their IEP/504

Meetings. Your child may not want to talk. Mine often tried to get me to speak for them. I was there to help, but I kept insisting that they speak for themselves. It was HARD for me to keep my mouth shut at times! When they turned 18, I let them handle their own meetings without me. They were able to do this because of the groundwork I had laid all the years before when I talked them through the process. The added benefit is that these are transferrable skills that they will carry with them through many situations in life, such as meetings with their managers at work and other conflict resolution situations.

There are parent advocacy groups that can help you navigate whatever you do not understand. Make use of them. Your son's entire future depends on paths that are laid out and decisions that are made very early in his school career.

CHAPTER 11
TEACH HIM TO TAKE CARE
OF HIMSELF

Teach him to take care of himself—cooking, cleaning, laundry, shopping, financial management, etc. You want him to be self-sufficient. These roles are not gender-specific. They're life skills, and everyone needs to learn them.

I admit that I'm not the best cook. I get by, but it's not something I truly enjoy. It's funny because I used to manage restaurants. Cooking in a corporate restaurant is very different from home-style cooking, though. After working extremely long hours in a restaurant, the last thing I wanted to do was to cook at home. Still, it was important for me to teach my sons how to shop for groceries, properly date and store foods, as well as monitoring proper food temperatures and cleaning procedures in the kitchen. They know how to cook for themselves without making themselves sick! At the same time, they also are really good at ordering takeout!

Tommy actually enjoys cooking, but I'm still working on his cleanliness. Progress, not perfection. Matt is my baking buddy.

Baking is actually something I love to do in the kitchen! When he was younger, he would help me measure and mix things, and he (like all kids) loved to lick the bowl. Those were really special times we shared. There are great math lessons included in measuring and reading recipes, and he was always proud of the items we baked. As he got older, he preferred to play his video games instead of helping me in the kitchen, but we still have great memories.

Sometimes, your son will burn items or ask questions about things that you think he should already know. That's okay. Answer his questions, and encourage his efforts. Trust me, I despise the mess that Tommy always makes in the kitchen… but I love it when he cooks so that I don't have to do it. It's a trade-off that works for us. I remember the first time Matt cooked spaghetti. I'm talking about just the noodles. The sauce was already made. He called me numerous times to make sure he was doing it right. The noodles weren't exactly like mine, but they were edible, and he felt a sense of accomplishment. Buy things that are easy for your son to cook on his own, even if they're not the healthiest choices. Boxed macaroni and cheese. Ramen noodles. Frozen meals. It will also take some of the pressure off of you.

Laundry is another valuable skill for your son to have. Teach him what products you use and why. Does he know how to sort his clothes? That's a great task for younger children who are learning their colors. Does he know how to put the soap in the washing machine? Let him help you by putting folded clothes away. Teach him how to fold them himself. It won't be perfect… don't expect it to be. He'll get better at it with practice. You can also teach him how to iron his own clothes and put them on hangers. The work and time you invest in teaching him these skills will pay off eventually.

When you go to the grocery store, let him pick certain items. When he is old enough not to be by your side, send him to get things from different aisles of the store and bring them back to you. That will shorten your trip and give him a sense of independence. In our house, they bring the groceries in, and I store them. They do know how to put them away, and sometimes I ask them to put the cold items in the refrigerator if I'm not able to get to it immediately. It's a shared responsibility. We're a team working together to keep our household functioning. When your son is old enough to drive, send him to the store to get a few things. It will be a long time before he feels comfortable doing the entire shopping, but he can take care of the quick lists. He may call you several times, and you may need to send him pictures or tell him which aisle has the item. Again, that's okay. It's all part of preparing him to be independent. This is also a great place to learn budgeting! Remember these are life skills.

Financial lessons are crucial. Although you don't want your son to worry about the financial pressure you may be facing, it is okay to share some things with him. For example, when it's time to go school shopping, give him a budget for the optional items. School supplies are important, and it's your job to figure out a way to get him what he needs. He also needs clothes and shoes. You can give him a budget and let him decide which clothes and shoes he wants. If he chooses that expensive pair of Nikes, then he needs to know that he will have fewer items because of that choice. Don't spend beyond your means. This can be difficult! When Matt started high school, he refused to wear Old Navy clothes anymore. I love Old

Navy, and I loved their prices! What I didn't realize was that wearing Old Navy (or any other inexpensive brand) was one of the many things that kids were using to pick on each other. This was hard, and there was no magic answer to it. You may find that reallocating where you spend your money can help. Another option is to buy things that serve a dual purpose. Matt loved "field swag" meaning really nice athletic wear for the football field. I bought him athletic wear that he could wear to school and on the field.

Let him earn the money needed for his extra-curricular activities. Band dues and football dues are expensive! Insist that he participate in all fundraisers. Tommy loved selling cookie dough every year, and he actually developed repeat customers for all of his fundraisers. This was a huge help in funding his band activities. We also worked the concession stand at a local arena together to earn money toward his dues. Matt participated in football fundraisers, but a lot less enthusiastically than his brother. In fact, Tommy usually ended up helping his brother. It was a family affair!

I didn't offer an allowance, but many mothers do. Decide if that is right for you and your family. If you do offer one, use it to help him manage his own money. Set up a youth checking account when he's old enough. It will be linked to yours, and you can monitor how he's managing his finances. Talk to him about what you're seeing. Hold him accountable, and teach him to take accountability for his actions. As soon as Matt turned 18, he wanted me to go to the bank to separate our bank accounts. I honored his wishes and felt confident in his ability to manage his money because of the discussions we had been having all along.

There are so many life lessons learned here that extend far beyond the initial goal. As mothers, our goal is to prepare our sons to be responsible, self-sufficient young men. Even if your son doesn't use these skills on a regular basis, you can rest assured knowing that you have taught him the skills. He's listening and watching, and when given the chance, he will amaze you with what he has learned and is able to do for himself!

CHAPTER 12
YOU ARE HIS EXAMPLE
OF A WOMAN

Remember that you are the most important person to set the example of how he views women, and your relationships will set the tone for how he will treat women in his life. This includes your relationship with him, as well as the people you date. Choose carefully who you bring home with you. Also, he is practicing every day with you. Accept nothing less than love and respect, and one day, you will notice that he has also become your protector and your biggest admirer!

Some things seem obvious. You've probably already heard things like letting him open doors for you. I personally didn't do much of that, because my son is not my man. We did talk about it, though, and what things a young man can do to treat a lady with respect. I believe these lessons are important regardless of gender identity and sexual orientation (his and/or yours). We'll talk about those very important and timely topics in another chapter.

For the sake of this chapter, let's talk about traditional female roles and how you can model what it means to be a woman. I believe it boils down to respecting yourself, respecting your son, and demanding (and commanding) his respect. Whom you date is your business. As a single woman, you may be looking for a new romantic interest. That's normal, and it's okay to allow yourself to explore your options. The key is to use discretion in deciding whether or not to allow someone to meet your son. I recommend waiting to do so. Take time and be absolutely certain that the person is someone you can trust to be around your son. Be sure that the person is someone you plan to date long-term. Your son will lose respect for you if he sees you making poor choices for yourself and if he sees you dating multiple people. Remember that I didn't say you can't date. I said your son doesn't need to see it until the relationship meets the threshold of long-term or even possible marriage potential.

You may wonder how that is possible when you don't have access to childcare, or if you already work long hours and don't want to spend any more time away from your son. It can be hard! I worked extremely long hours as a restaurant manager, causing my sons to spend an extraordinary amount of time in childcare. Not only did I not want them to have babysitters when I wasn't working, but I also couldn't afford anything more than I was already paying for. This is where I got creative. I planned our living space so that there was enough distance between my room and theirs to allow some degree of privacy. My room was also by the front door, so I would hear if someone knocked on the door without disturbing them. It was necessary for me to plan the visits late at night or during the day when I had a weekday off, while they were at school. Once they were old enough to be at home alone, I began to allow myself date nights. These never included overnight stays until they were adults.

As hard as you try, you may fall short of the standards you set for yourself. You may introduce someone to your son who you are certain is "the one" yet he turns out not to be. I once made the mistake of introducing someone to Tommy and Matt shortly after we had begun dating. I thought he was a nice guy, and they were older. I thought it would be okay. It wasn't. He had a very short fuse, and he got angry quickly. He never hit me. I don't even think he yelled a lot, but there were fits of jealousy and something about him that my sons picked up on even before I had had enough. They told me that they thought something was wrong with him, and they didn't want me dating him. I had to be honest with myself and listen to what they were saying. I ended the relationship. I think the fact that I listened to them and made the right decision helped to turn around what could have had a very negative impact on their opinion of me. Had I kept dating him, they likely would have lost respect for me because they would have seen me as not respecting myself or them.

My sons have always paid close attention to the way I dress, the way I do my hair and makeup, and even the fact that I always keep a fresh pedicure. Take pride in your appearance when you go up to your son's school. Wear tasteful clothes, even when dressed casually. Trust me, I didn't dress up for football games or volunteering, but I always made sure I looked presentable. It's important for them to see you as a woman who respects and takes care of herself. When I look at the girls that Matthew likes, they usually have similar qualities as me. It's clear that he has shaped his expectations of women based on the example I have set. Tommy doesn't date women, but he is equally proud of me as his mom. He loves to tell me that his friends think I'm a "hottie." I just laugh because I don't see myself that way at all. It is flattering to hear, though.

Your son will observe the way you carry yourself. He'll also be watching both the way you interact with others and the way you interact with him. Let your actions support the standards you have set for him. I already talked to you about speaking love and life into him. That's a given. You can teach him to be a man of his word by being a woman of your word. Be someone he can trust. Demand that he speaks to you with respect, even when he gets older and his voice starts to change. Especially, then. I can't tell you how many times I asked Matt and Tommy, *"Who are you talking to?"* or said, *"Don't raise your voice at me,"* or *"Don't use that bass in your voice when you're talking to me."* If I hear Matt on the phone talking rudely to a girl, I talk to him about it. Let your son know that he can express his feelings and opinions without speaking rudely or cursing or demeaning someone.

Work hard, and talk to him about your goals. He will learn his work ethic from you. If you want him to respect women as equals, show him what that looks like. You don't have to be cynical or angry. Just be an example of a woman who works hard and accomplishes what she sets out to accomplish in life. Go back to school and further your education, if that's important to you. I went back to college and got my Bachelor's Degree. I did it for myself initially, but the pride and excitement they shared with me were priceless! When I got promoted to General Manager, they were ecstatic… because they knew how hard I worked, and I had shared my goal with them at each step along the way. It was something we accomplished together. Their sacrifice of time with me and their cooperation with their babysitter and teachers made it possible for me to invest in having a better life for us. Writing this book is another huge goal that I shared with them. We discussed the deadlines that I set for myself, and I shared each chapter with them. It was important for me to get their approval because I'm sharing our story, not just mine. Seeing you set goals and accomplish them will show him that women are capable, intelligent, and strong. By earning his respect, you are teaching him to respect women as a whole. That is a big part of what will make him not just a man, but a gentleman.

CHAPTER 13
TALK TO HIM ABOUT SEX, SEXUAL ORIENTATION, & GENDER IDENTITY

Talk to him about sex. He won't want to talk to you but do it anyway. Start early with age-appropriate explanations. A penis is a penis. Let him know that it is normal for him to touch it. It's his, after all, but that's a private matter. In my house, my sons understand that private matters should be handled in their bedrooms or in the bathroom—NOT in common areas.

Speaking of private matters, once a boy is toilet trained and able to safely bathe himself, there is no need for his mother to be in the bathroom with him. Respect his privacy. If there is a problem with his genitals, he will let you know. At that point, you will need to let him know that you need to look at it and/or touch it and then ASK PERMISSION before proceeding. Make sure his doctor also asks permission before examining him. When he gets older, you may also want to excuse yourself during the actual examination and return to talk to the doctor afterward. It's a judgment call. Make sure that you and your son trust the doctor. You could even discuss with your son before the appointment whether or not he would prefer for you to step out of the room. This will show him the importance of personal boundaries and consent. It will enable him to tell anyone (even you) that it is not okay to touch him. What a powerful lesson!

Do not walk around the house naked, and don't allow him to do so either. Insist that he knocks before entering your room, and show him the same courtesy. You may want to get into the habit of locking your door when you are dressing. Even with rules about knocking, they forget sometimes, and you can avoid embarrassing situations. I once had a late-night guest… long after my kids were asleep. I forgot to lock my bedroom door, and Tommy walked in. I was mortified! I assure you I never made that mistake again.

If there is a male in his life who can talk to him about sex, sexuality, and all the other issues that adolescents face today, great… but understand that this does not free you of the responsibility to talk to him, too. It is extremely important that you LISTEN during these conversations, and know your child. You don't want to over-talk the matter, but he needs to know that you are a safe person when he needs you… and that you will help him through these very difficult years. Coaches, priests/pastors, youth ministers, older brothers can all be excellent resources, but they are supplements not substitutes for you. Know what he is learning from others and be his translator, and by all means, correct any misinformation he has received. You will be amazed at the things he will hear outside your home!

You can share your ideas and standards with your son, but don't assume he will follow them. This simply means that you might hope he will wait to have sex, but he may not. It's your job to make sure he knows how to keep himself safe no matter what he decides. In other words, buy condoms for him. Take him to buy them with you or just buy them and give them to him at home. This is an opportunity to have a conversation. Tell him that the expectation is that if he does choose to have sex, he needs to make wise choices that will protect his health and his life… and of course to prevent unwanted pregnancy. Most young men want to experiment sexually, including without protection. They think they're invincible, and their confidence in the withdrawal method is astounding. Keep talking to him, and make sure the condoms are available. The rest is up to him. I knew that Tommy had been listening to my conversations about sexual health and safety when he announced that he wanted to go on "Prep," which is a medication to protect from HIV. I had never heard of it. He had done his own research about how to keep himself safe, and I felt a sense of relief knowing that he was taking responsibility for his own health. Of course, I told him that he still needed to use condoms!

A word about sexual orientation and gender identity. Your child is the same person you fell in love with the day they were born. Whether they like boys, girls, or both. Whether they want to wear pants or dresses. Whether they identify as gay, straight, male, female, non-binary, or somewhere in-between. Your job is still to love your child just the way they are. I don't even like the word "accept" in this context, because it can be perceived as accepting something that would not be considered okay. Love is an action word. Love them. Period. I'm intentionally using non-binary pronouns here because I truly believe this with all of my being. Talk to your child and find out who they are… also, what and who are important to them.

For years, I suspected that Tommy was gay. He never commented on it, though. I decided to ask questions and lay the framework so that he would feel safe telling me when he was ready. I would ask, *"Do you have a girlfriend...or a boyfriend?"* Then I would assure him that either would be fine with me. I just wanted him to be happy. We were very open about these conversations at home. Nothing was hidden. Matt and I would talk about it sometimes, not to talk about Tommy, but it was important to me to make sure Matt was also a safe person for Tommy. I'm so glad I did because Tommy came out as gay to Matt long before he did to me! My conversations with him today revolve around healthy relationships. I want him to find love or rather love to find him. I would be thrilled if he chooses to marry someday! I tell him that it's possible and gay men can have children too. Gotta put that plug in for my potential grandchildren! Words cannot express the joy I feel in my heart when Tommy brings his friends home to meet me. He's proud to have a mom who loves him for who he is, and I'm happy to extend that love to his friends. He's also very clear that he is a "dude." I respect that, and that's why I use the pronouns he has chosen.

I encourage you to please have honest and open conversations with your child. Find out what's important to them and how they see themself. You've already built a solid foundation with all the love you've been pouring into them and the lessons you've taught them about how to make decisions. Trust their instinct and respect what they tell you, even if it is not what you had hoped for them. Pay close attention, and you will probably see signs. Don't put blinders on and ignore those signs. Grieve if you need to grieve your idea of what you thought your child would be. Then get over it and keep on loving the unique person they have always been.

CHAPTER 14
MAN OF THE HOUSE—
OR NOT?!

When I first got divorced, Tommy asked me if he could be my husband, since his father wasn't going to be my husband anymore. At the time, it was cute... funny, even. Imagine a seven-year-old boy looking me in the eye, sincerely wanting to be my husband! Between the two of them, my sons have alternated between assuming the roles of husband, father, guardian, protector... they never saw themselves as little boys. I took my responsibility to protect them from growing up before their time very seriously. They were children—my sons. While I taught them what it means to be a man and encouraged them to aspire to be the best men they can be, I also fiercely protected their childhood.

We're cuddlers in our house... all of us. Co-sleepers from birth, I had to deliberately kick them out of my room and my bed when they reached adolescence. Matt gives great massages. He actually has gifted hands... healing hands. Yet I had to refrain from allowing him to massage my aching shoulders and back. These are innocent examples of acts that could blur the lines for little boys and mothers, especially, in the absence of a man in the household. These young men are still my sons, and I have a responsibility to keep clear boundaries in order to prevent any inappropriate or confusing issues that could contribute to them developing an Oedipus complex.

I kept my personal dating life private for years. However, it wasn't a matter of secrecy. My youngest frequently made statements designed to make me feel guilty about not sharing my personal business with him. He even threatened to keep secrets from me about his life in retaliation. The fact of the matter is that I am an adult. Secrets can be dangerous for children, and I had a responsibility to know what was going on in my young children's lives. There is a fine line between respecting their privacy and not paying attention. I also refused to allow that kind of emotional manipulation.

There is no need to introduce every potential romantic interest to your children. Allow yourself the time and space to date without the obligation of having to explain if things don't work out. Anyone I introduce to my kids will have made it through the initial stages of getting to know each other. He will be someone I plan to have around for the long term. The last thing they need is to see a revolving door of men in and out of my life. That would be confusing for them and could also be a source of disrespect for them towards me… and ultimately, to all women.

Another thing to consider is how you introduce your love interest to your child. Whether male or female, look for someone who respects and cares about your son. I'm speaking here of men because that's my personal experience. The principles still apply regardless of gender. The gentleman I'm dating now waited years before meeting my sons. Truthfully, I was ready for him to meet them long before he was. When they were going through puberty, I longed for someone to be present on a regular basis who could be a role model, and support me in parenting. Looking back, I'm glad we waited. Our relationship is much stronger than it was then, and it shows. That is a big factor in their ability to accept him into my life.

Even once he met them, he only had minimal conversations with them at first. They were in their late teens and early twenties by then. He told me that they were grown men, and he treated them as such. It took time, but they warmed up to him *because* he respected them and their feelings, and their place in our home. There were no power struggles or even competition for my attention. They each now have their own unique relationship with him, based on mutual respect. He never demanded it—he earned it.

Use your judgment. Talk to your partner before introducing them to your son. Make sure that their approach is one that will be respectful of your son and his feelings. Talk to your son before bringing someone home. It's not fair to surprise him and expect him to respond politely. Answer his questions within reason, and set expectations about his behavior. He needs to be polite and bring any concerns to you directly. Showing concern for his feelings and opinions will go a long way toward facilitating a positive relationship between him and your mate.

Be patient. Don't look to every person you date as a possible substitute for your son's father. It's natural to want a co-parent in the household with you, especially, if his dad is not actively involved in his life. Remember that it's best to approach parenting as if you are the only one responsible for your child. Any help you get is a bonus. That doesn't mean it won't happen. It may. Let it happen organically.

Don't force it. Be certain that you're making a good *parenting* decision by bringing someone new into your son's life. If not, you can still date the person… just keep it separate from your son.

The reality is that your son will see himself as the man of the house. If you have more than one son, they will likely see it as a shared responsibility. They're technically right. At least, they're the men *in* the house. I've learned to respect my children's feelings. Allowing him to accept age-appropriate household responsibilities will teach your son many qualities that are expected of and admired in men. You're in essence teaching him what I've been talking about all along—how to be a gentleman.

What I've come to realize is that there is a difference between being the man of the house and being my man. That's not a son's role, and I deserve to have someone in my life who fulfills my needs as a woman that no child can fill.

CHAPTER 15
TEACH HIM ABOUT
MALCOLM X

Teach him about Malcolm X. He'll learn about Dr. Martin Luther King, Jr. in school, but they won't tell him about Malcolm... or they'll only tell part of the story.

If you haven't read it yourself, I highly recommend you read *THE AUTOBIOGRAPHY OF MALCOLM X*, As Written by Alex Haley. The movie "Malcolm X," starring Denzel Washington, is a must-watch too. It's never too late. I didn't read Malcolm's auto-biography until it was required reading at my beloved HBCU (Historically Black College/University—Aggie Pride!). It was truly an eye-opening experience for me. No matter how hard I tried, and believe me, I did, my children did not inherit my love of reading. Getting them to read the book for pleasure was not going to hap-pen. I did, however, get Matt to watch the movie with me. He didn't choose it, but he did enjoy watching it with me. Try sharing one or the other with your son.

Aside from the obvious, setting the record straight about who Malcolm X was and what he represented, I believe his message was an important one of what it means to be a man. His message coincides with the lessons I have been working very hard to instill in Tommy and Matt. I absolutely believe in the importance of education, lifelong learning, standing up for what I believe is right, and the self-love he preached and encouraged all Black people to embrace. These are universal truths, regardless of religious affiliation. I believe there is an important lesson therein and of itself… that we can learn from those who may believe differently than we do. By teaching your son to listen with an open mind and to discern for himself what is right and true for him, you are giving him an invaluable gift.

As a little boy, Malcolm's teacher told him that he couldn't be a lawyer, because of his race. That teacher also told him that a carpenter would be a more suitable career for him. Young Malcolm believed that teacher and set his dream aside. He was a brilliant student, yet this one teacher discouraged him. He then used his mind to con others, to outsmart them in dishonest ways. Those ways caught up with him, and he went to prison. A fellow prisoner saw something special in Malcolm and taught him the importance of the written word, of educating himself. He taught those lessons in conjunction with introducing Malcolm to Islam. I believe that Islam was the mechanism that brought out what was already in Malcolm. He was a star, destined to shine. A natural leader. When Malcolm opened himself to using his gifts for good, he changed the lives of many and the trajectory of a nation. I believe this is an example of God's grace… no matter what name you call God.

You see, both parts of Malcolm X's story are important. Even the X is important. The X in mathematics is used to name the unknown. It is paying respect to what was lost when our ancestors were brought to this country. Something as simple and as powerful as our family names. I want my sons to know that they get to choose their destiny. They get to define who they are and what they want to be in life. They don't have to take on the prejudices of others and make it their reality. I want to teach them to take responsibility for their choices. I want them to know that it is never too late for them to choose a different path.

Malcolm X also learned a painful lesson about blind loyalty. He was completely devoted to the Honorable Elijah Muhammad, his mentor and the leader of his faith. It devastated him when he learned about his leader's transgressions. This is a valuable lesson for any young man. It's an example of what I was talking about earlier regarding not letting your son be a "yes" man and teaching him to think for himself. In speaking of this, Malcolm said, *"To me, the thing that is worse than death is betrayal. You see, I could conceive death, but I could not conceive betrayal."*

Here are a few more quotes from Malcolm X that I believe define what it means to be a man:

"A man who stands for nothing will fall for anything."

"You're not to be so blind with patriotism that you can't face reality. Wrong is wrong, no matter who does it or says it."

"I have often reflected upon the new vistas that reading has opened to me... As I see it today, the ability to read awoke inside me some long dormant craving to be mentally alive."

"We cannot think of being acceptable to others until we have first proven acceptable to ourselves."

"Children have a lesson adults should learn, to not be ashamed of failing, but to get up and try again."

"Despite my firm convictions, I have been always a man who tries to face facts, and to accept the reality of life as new experience and new knowledge unfolds it. I have always kept an open mind, which is necessary to the flexibility that must go hand in hand with every form of intelligent search for truth."

"Hatred and anger are powerless when met with kindness."

"One day, may we all meet together in the light of understanding."

I'm always impressed by Malcolm's evolution, by his commitment to his education, and by his willingness to reinvent himself based on his ever-expanding worldview. You don't have to be a Muslim to agree with the message that he was preaching to Black men about what it means to be a man and a father. This is just as relevant today as it was then! Malcolm was also a living example of a man who took responsibility for his own actions, beliefs, and behavior. I do not strive to raise perfect men. My goal is to raise men who have the ability and the willingness to think for themselves, learn from their mistakes, and speak unashamedly up for what they believe to be right. I have yet to come across a better example of these qualities than the true-life example of Malcolm X!

CHAPTER 16
TEACH HIM
ABOUT FRIENDSHIP

Teach him how to choose his friends and how to be a friend. Years ago, when I first started writing this book, I tried to summarize my thoughts on friendship for two days. I have a tendency to overcomplicate things, and that is definitely not what I want for this book. I decided to ask Matt what I had taught him about friendship (I highly recommend asking your son what lessons you have taught him. It can be very enlightening to hear how he has perceived all that you have told and shown him). This is what Matt told me:

"How do you choose your friends? You choose a friend that you can trust and who can also push you to be a better person, and who will keep you out of trouble."

"How to be a good friend? You be there for your friend when they need help/advice. Be someone they can count on and push them to the best of their abilities."

It's moments like these that let me know he has heard and incorporated all the lessons I've tried to share with him into who he is… and I am so very proud of him! The other things he said during our discussion but did not write down were that if your friends are doing something they shouldn't be doing, tell them to stop. If they don't, just leave. Don't get caught up in a bad situation just because your friends are doing the wrong thing. He understands the concept of guilt by association, yet he doesn't deny friendship to children due to unfair and/or inaccurate labels, which have been placed on them by authority figures. There is good in everyone, and he may be the one person who helps someone see the good in themselves, and to give them the confidence to be the person that God intended them to be.

There is a delicate balancing act required of our Black sons. I would be negligent if I didn't tell Tommy and Matt the story of Jordan Davis, who was murdered while sitting unarmed in the back seat of his friend's car simply because the music was too loud for another patron of the same gas station. I don't want them to be fearful, but I do want them to be wise. They are both well-liked and have the ability to reason with people and even to mediate. My concern is that they may one day try to negotiate with someone who cannot be reached… and who may be armed and dangerous. I try to teach them to be good and loyal friends and wise observers of people so that they can make a difference in the lives of others while also protecting their own lives.

Sometimes, it's difficult to have these conversations. Keep trying. It's a very tall order, and it requires vigilance, open lines of communication, and a lot of prayer on a daily basis. Both Tommy and Matt have each come to me on different occasions to ask for advice or to share something they have been dealing with in their friendships. Your son will too, as long as you keep talking to him and letting him know that you are always ready and willing to listen without judgment.

Tommy had a harder time making friends due to the social challenges he faced that were associated with autism. I'm a musician, and I know that being in a band or any musical ensemble creates a special dynamic where friendships are forged through shared experiences. When he started middle school, I gave him a choice between band and chorus. He had previously sung in the Atlanta Boy Choir briefly as a young member of the Apprentice Choir. I knew he loved singing and had a natural musical ability. He chose band, and it was a life-changing experience for him! It's amazing how just by making one conscious choice to encourage your child, other opportunities and benefits unfold beyond your imagination. Being in the band, Tommy made friends that he would not have otherwise had. It gave him self-confidence. He was a talented trombonist! I also believe that playing the trombone helped him by providing the oral self-stimulation that he craved to calm his anxieties and had previously only met by chewing on bottle caps, pencils, and all sorts of inappropriate things that were harmful to his teeth. Back to the friendships he gained… this one entry into the arts also opened doors for him to explore theater. In the theater, he learned how to read facial expressions and how to understand voice intonation. Those lessons helped him form friendships in a way that had previously been extremely difficult due to his autism.

This is an example of one of the things you can proactively do to help your son make friends without choosing his friends for him or forcing him into uncomfortable situations. Pay attention to his interests and gifts, and let that be your guide.

That same unconditional love you have shown your son will show up in his friendships. It gives me great joy to see both Tommy and Matt speak up to their friends when they don't agree with their choices. They speak their minds and do it in a way that shows they care about their friends. They are able to preserve their friendships through really difficult situations. Their friends know that they can count on them to be truthful, trustworthy, and loyal.

I believe that lessons in friendship really revolve around integrity. A gentleman stands up for what he believes in; speaks truthfully, even when the truth is hard to hear, is loyal, admits when he is wrong, and always strives to do better the next time. These same traits carry over into what will make your son a good business partner, husband, father, and overall human being.

Matt also told me recently that he appreciates the impact that growing up with Tommy has had on him. He remembers the lessons that I taught him when his brother was first diagnosed on the autism spectrum… about how to have compassion and to look at his brother's heart and not always mind the hurtful things Tommy sometimes said to him. He says he understands the importance of not hitting below the belt and tries to live by that standard. He was animated when telling me this… passionate even. There is nothing more gratifying than hearing your son tell you how much he values the lessons you have taught him. Keep talking to your son. Share examples with him of you being a friend to your own friends and siblings. He is listening, and one day you will hear him speaking the same words you have spoken to him. Even better, you will witness him living out those same values with his own friends.

CHAPTER 17
HELP HIM TO FIND
HIS PURPOSE

Everybody has a purpose in life. As stated in Chapter Four, everyone has a gift. Our gifts are what give us a window to see our purpose in life. It is easy as parents to fall into the trap of pushing our children into our own dreams for them. We want them to be successful, to have a better life than us. Sometimes, we even push them to fulfill our own unfulfilled dreams for ourselves. None of these will make them happy or give them a sense of fulfilment. The key is to focus on their God-given gifts… and to LISTEN when they tell us what they want for themselves.

Watch your son as he is doing the things he loves. What makes his face light up? If he is irresponsible with all other responsibilities, what is the one thing he never ever misses? For my oldest son, it was music and drama in school. As brilliant as he is in Math and Science, it was still like pulling teeth to get assignments turned in on time… even in Calculus and Physics. This is the same child who scored a 675 on the Math portion of his SAT without studying at all. He's great at it, but he doesn't love it. Yet if you talked to his

Band Director, the Orchestra Director who worked with him on several special projects, or our church Choir Director who asked him to learn to play a second instrument in order to accompany us at Christmas, they would all tell you that there is not one thing they asked of him that he didn't do... extremely well.

I have to admit that it's frightening for me to think of him hanging his entire future on a dream to be an actor or a musician. This has been a balancing act for me. The reality is that the reason he discovered his passion for the arts is that I have always provided opportunities for him to participate in the arts. Okay, I must give credit first to my mother who encouraged me to let him audition for the Atlanta Boy Choir when he was about five years old. We had to do something... he had every single episode of "Barney" memorized—lyrics, dialogue, dances, everything!

As he approached high school graduation, I wanted desperately for him to do something which would enable him to make a good living and to provide for himself and for his family. Finally, I came to the realization that he didn't have to make a final decision right then. What a relief that was for both of us! We considered a military career at one point, thinking that a military environment would be great for him since he has autism and would benefit from the structure provided by the military. The military also has phenomenal opportunities for musicians via military bands. He took the Armed Services Vocational Aptitude Battery (ASVAB). His score was exceptionally high! It was so high that he was recommended for a top security clearance level analyst-type position. I was excited about the possibilities this would open up for him! In fact, I was probably more excited than he was if I'm being honest. He was all set to enlist, and the last thing he had to do was pass the physical exam. Well, during that exam, he told them about his autism. He didn't realize that autism is in the list of causes for automatic disqualification from military service. He was both disappointed and a bit relieved. I felt the same way. He had already decided that college wasn't for him. I felt like this was such a huge blow to his chances for a viable career. Yet I also felt relieved. There was a part of me that had been worried. Worried that I had pushed him into doing something that he didn't really want to do… something that could ultimately get him killed. I didn't want to carry the responsibility for such a life-and-death decision. This experience taught me that my job is to support his dreams and aspirations without imposing my wishes on him.

My response to Tommy was to assure him that everything would work out. He had time to figure out what he wanted to do with his life. In the meantime, he had two choices. Go to school or get a job. Period. That is what a responsible young man does. He sets goals for himself, and he carries his weight in the family and in the world. He began working in fast food and eventually got a job as a server. He LOVES the money he makes as a server, as well as the freedom he has to do what he wants when he wants. It has turned out to be a good fit for him. He also has the flexibility to explore his other interests. He has done some work as an extra for TV shows that are filmed locally. Most recently, he started taking voiceover classes. This is something I suggested he might enjoy when I began exploring my own career as a voice actor. He's just starting on his voiceover journey and is excited about the possibilities.

For his twenty-fifth birthday, I gave Tommy tickets to see "Hamilton." He loved it! It was a reminder for him of how much he loves the theater. We talked about the various opportunities there are in our area for free training programs in things like set design and various other theater-related careers. He sounded interested, but it will be up to him to follow through on his interest.

When Matthew was young, he loved football, and he was really good at it! As he got older, he became discouraged because of the politics associated with football. He missed his eighth-grade season because I didn't have the money to pay by the deadline. I contacted the Football Director at the park before the deadline to ask if I could pay the following week, and he told me they were not accepting late registrations. This was a pivotal year, and I believe it had a detrimental effect on his high school career. Football was never the same for him. I encouraged him to stick with it. *"Life lessons are learned on the football field,"* I told him. It's true. He learned how to deal with adversity, how to be a supportive teammate, how to keep showing up when life is hard. Still, his dreams of playing college football never materialized.

I gave Matt the same choices I gave his brother: Go to school or get a job. I encouraged non-traditional forms of education, too. There are so many lucrative careers that do not require a Bachelor's Degree. Electricians, plumbers, barbers, HVAC technicians, etc. all make great money along with the option to own their own businesses. I felt this would be great for Matt since he has a true entrepreneurial spirit. Tommy tried to talk him into working in the restaurant business, but Matt was very clear that he is not interested in serving. He chose a job in retail, and he enrolled in a local four-year university.

He tried it out for two semesters and decided it isn't for him at this time. We looked at an online IT certification. He says he intends to complete it but hasn't made much progress on that yet. I continue to support him without pressuring him. It's a delicate balance. He also worked (briefly) at FedEx but decided that unloading trucks was definitely not for him. Most recently, he started working at a telecommunications company. It's a job he has wanted for a while, and he didn't stop until he was hired. He loves the hours and the money he is making. He also has time to enjoy his social interests and to try acting.

Both Tommy and Matt are happy right now, and I see that as a success for them and for me as their mother. We haven't landed on what either of them sees as their true purpose in life, but they'll keep trying. They also have the skills to go after their dreams. They have the courage to try new things and to get back up when faced with rejection. Their self-esteem is intact, and they are both really wonderful young men who have a positive impact on everyone they meet. I think as humans, we all share that one very important purpose—to use our gifts, talents, and humanity to make the world a better, kinder place.

When all is said and done, your son will be the one living with his decisions. Your job is to help him to find his purpose—NOT to tell him what you think his purpose is and to force him into being what you think he should be. If you have helped him to recognize his gifts, made him aware of the options available to him to support and use his gifts, as well as taught him well how to pray and to listen for guidance, and to trust his own instincts, then you will have done your part in helping him to find his own purpose.

CHAPTER 18
LET HIM GO

It isn't possible to be with our children 24/7. The goal is to teach them to know the difference between right and wrong, to solve their own problems, and to ask for help when needed. I often tell my sons that I have taught them right from wrong. I may not know what they are doing, but at any given time, they will always know... and so will God. The God I know is not looking to catch us doing things wrong or testing us. I don't say this to them in order to instill fear. The point is that they have to be able to look themselves in the mirror every day... and hopefully, they can do so knowing that they have done their best.

Letting go is hard, especially when you consider the "Two Strikes" rule. There is a part of me that worries every time they walk out the door. Yet I can't stop them from living their lives and making their own choices. There was a time when I would call or text them repeatedly when they were out. When they were younger, I could keep track of who they were with, where they were going, and whether or not any parents were going to be there. I knew all of their friends and their friends' parents.

As they got older, I tried discussing things with them before they left the house. I asked where they were going and talked about different scenarios. "What will you do if…" and encouraged them to develop a plan for what to do if things went wrong. I made sure they always had working cell phones. I can't imagine how parents of my generation felt when we left home without cell phones or any way to reach us!

The key is to have age-appropriate accountability and trust. Hopefully, you have developed trust with your son before he starts driving, dating, going to parties, etc. That trust goes two ways. You need to be able to trust him, and he needs to be able to trust that he can come to you with ANY problem he has and that you will support him through it. If you want him to be honest with you, don't overreact when he tells you the truth. Take a deep breath and work towards a solution together with him.

When it comes to accountability, set the expectation that he will answer your calls and/or texts. This requires flexibility, though, and some self-accountability. I used to get so frustrated when Matt ignored my calls. I had to realize that I was calling him too much… and not for important reasons. My anxiety was getting in my own way. He also asked me one day to text him instead of calling. He said it was easier for him to respond to a text than a phone call. Young men don't want their friends knowing their mommy is checking on them! I decided to honor his request and text whenever possible.

What do I mean by "age-appropriate" accountability? A 14-year-old requires more supervision. At that age, I wanted to know the address of where they were going, who was going to be there, and I had to have a conversation with a parent who was going to be there. A ride home with someone meant I had to know the parent (or teammate) who was driving. When my sons were 16, I still wanted to know what time they would be home and what their plans were in general, but I didn't have to know every detail. I also didn't insist on speaking directly with a parent, especially, if I knew and trusted the parent. Matt was driving at 16. Tommy decided he wasn't ready to drive until he was 18. It would have been a lot easier for me if he had his license, but I really admired the fact that he knew he wasn't ready. When Matt started driving, I knew that he sometimes gave friends and teammates rides, and I factored that time into my expectations for when he should be home. By the time they were 18, I talked to them and encouraged them to make wise decisions. My parting words whenever they left home were, "Be safe, and make wise decisions!" I knew that I had taught them to think for themselves, and it was time for me to trust them to use those skills. Now that they are both in their twenties, I simply remind them to be safe... and of course, I always tell them how much I love them! I knew I had made a big stride in letting go when instead of texting, "Where are you?" I began texting, "Are you safe?" A "Yes" answer allowed me to put my mind at ease and get a good night's sleep, even if they weren't home yet. This has worked extremely well for us!

Letting go is a gradual process. You don't just wake up one day and stop worrying or checking up on your son. That's not realistic or healthy. Let your son know that his actions and behavior will help him earn your trust and his own independence. By letting go gradually, you also build up your own tolerance and significantly reduce your anxiety. You may not like every choice he makes, but you still have to allow your son to make choices and decisions for himself. I tell Tommy and Matt that it's up to them to decide what kind of people they are going to be. I will always love them and support them and help them in any way I can. They understand that to be a man means to be accountable for and to oneself. It's about integrity, which can be defined as doing the right thing—even when no one else is watching.

CHAPTER 19
FORGIVE YOURSELF

Once you have done your best, forgive yourself for the mistakes, choices, and decisions you have made and will make. Motherhood is a journey. There will be bumps on the road, detours, inclement weather... but there will also be sunshine, scenic roads, shared experiences, and precious memories. I've tried to present a reasonable, accurate picture of my mothering journey with you. My goal has been to share the ups and downs, my victories, and my stumbles along the way. In fact, I approached this book with the mindset that it could help someone *because* I'm not a doctor or other childcare professional. I'm you. Years ago, I was where you are right now. Years from now, you will be looking back as I am today. What will you say? How will you feel? Will you give yourself grace?

One of my biggest regrets is the time I spent away from my sons while I was working in the restaurant business. I believed it was a necessary choice in order to provide for them. The toll it took on my health cannot be denied. I was stressed literally all the time. Who would care for them? How could I get Saturdays off for Matt's little league football games? What about Friday nights so I could see

Tommy march in the band under the lights at his high school football games? When they were old enough to stay home alone, could I trust them to be responsible? I certainly needed the financial relief of not having to pay for childcare.

One day, I was home on my day off when a social worker from Children and Family Services knocked on my door. Tommy was in middle school, and Matt was in elementary school. Matt got home from school one hour before Tommy did. This was a dilemma for me because I was usually at work. I had made the difficult decision to allow Matt to stay at home alone for that one hour before the babysitter came to pick them both up and take them to her house. She lived in a different school district, so they weren't able to ride the bus to her house. Extended hours of childcare is extremely difficult to find, and she was wonderful. Apparently, a neighbor had reported to Children and Family Services that my children were left unattended in the afternoon. I was terrified that I would lose my sons! Thankfully, I spoke up for myself. I explained my situation to her, including the fact that I didn't qualify for financial assistance and was doing the best I could. She completed her investigation and closed the case, but it definitely caused me to question my own ability to take care of my children.

Believe me when I say that no matter how much preparation you do, no matter how hard you try to protect your son, things are going to happen that you don't expect or condone. It wasn't until many years later that Tommy and Matt told me stories of how they spent their afternoons when I had just been promoted to General Manager and had decided to allow Tommy to watch his little brother. He had turned 13 by then, so legally he was considered old enough to babysit Matt. We lived in a second-floor apartment. They literally played games where they would jump off the balcony and climb back up! Tommy locked Matt and his friend out on the balcony, and they jumped down and went around to the front door to let themselves back in. I was mortified when I heard this, just thinking of how dangerous this was! They, on the other hand, laugh every time they talk about it. I'm grateful that they survived. I can't change what happened, so I give myself grace and thank God for protecting them.

There were times when I simply didn't have money to buy the gifts or clothes or the school supplies that they needed. I'm so very grateful for our church family and our close friends who stepped in without being asked to fill in the gaps for them and for me. It was a humbling experience for me, but I learned to swallow my pride and accept the help that was offered with much gratitude.

There will also be situations that are completely beyond your control. I remember being hospitalized for four days with a migraine headache that was also made much worse by leaking spinal fluid. This "spinal" headache literally made me feel like I was going to die. It brought up fears of dying and not being there for my sons. We had no family living near us, and we had only lived there for a few years. Thankfully, I had created a village around us with a neighbor who was the grandmother of one of their friends, and another friend whose son played football with Matt. They stepped up and played a significant role in making sure that my sons were cared for while I was away.

I have several chronic health conditions. I've always done my best to take care of them, including my depression. What I didn't know is that I'm actually bipolar. A few years ago, I was in an acute manic stage and was suffering from delusions brought on by the mania. Tommy was so concerned by my behavior that he called my family as well as 911. I remember being wheeled out on a stretcher and seeing our neighbor coming to check on us. All I could say to her was, "Please, take care of my children!" She assured me that she would. She and that same friend I mentioned previously worked together to make sure they were taken care of—physically and emotionally.

Speaking of mental and emotional health, be aware that your son may feel some anxiety and sadness simply because he picks up on your stress level. Matt is very sensitive to my emotions, even when I don't speak of them. He has gone through periods of melancholy because of it, and he refused to talk to me about it, because he feared upsetting me. I tried my best to put on a brave face around my sons, but the downside of being so close is that they can read me as well as I can read them. He still talks about a time when he was outside at night when I had just gotten home. I didn't see him coming up to the car, and I was crying. It affected him deeply to see me crying in the car before I went inside to be with him and Tommy. He felt sadness, but I also think he gained an understanding and compassion for me, and all I was trying to do for them. He also felt responsible for me and a need to make sure I was okay. You're not going to be able to shield your son from experiencing any pain at all. However, if you have done the work to build his coping skills and to strengthen your relationship with him, he will get through the pain. If his sadness is overwhelming or lasting for a long time, please get him counseling. The same goes for you. If your burden feels too heavy, reach out for help.

I'm sharing these painful memories with you so that you will know that you are not alone. Don't expect perfection from yourself. Build your support system to fill in those gaps for you. Don't be too proud to admit when you need help. Be open and honest with your son, in an age-appropriate way. As hard as you try to hide it, he knows when you are stressed or not well. I'm not suggesting that you lay all your burdens on him. He isn't your therapist. What you can say is that you're getting help and assure him that things will be okay. Let him know that you will always do your best to make sure he is safe. Seeing you work through your struggles and overcome them will be the best example he needs to believe that he can overcome his own struggles too. No mother wants her child to see her hitting rock-bottom. Remember that it's not weakness. You're human.

These are just a few of the mistakes I've made and the challenges we've faced. At times, I still feel regret. During my best moments, I understand that the challenges we've faced together, along with each of our mistakes, have all worked to help us build a bond that can never be broken. I look at Tommy and Matt, and I feel the depth of our love for each other. That's where I find the strength to forgive myself.

CHAPTER 20
SHARE YOUR BELIEFS
WITH HIM

Whatever your belief system may be, it is more important than ever for you to immerse yourself in it. A community of those who share your values and beliefs will uplift you and your children, and support you through the most difficult times. You will also be a blessing to the community. Don't deprive yourself, your sons, or the community of all that you were meant to be to each other.

I intentionally said "belief system" rather than faith. That's because I don't want religion to be a barrier that prevents anyone from hearing the message I'm trying to convey here. We all have values that are important to us. What are your values? What is your moral compass? Is God important to you? Is right and wrong important to you? What about love, compassion, integrity, and hope? Wherever you find your guideposts in life, share that with your son. Do you pray? If so, pray without ceasing for him. If not, do you believe in the law of attraction and positive affirmations? Are you spiritual or religious or both? Do you believe words have power? Speak life and love over your son. Just know that whatever you believe, you must share it in a *non-judgmental, life-affirming* way.

If you're a religious person and you want your son to share your religion, don't use that religion to shame him or to try to change him. Use it to inspire and uplift him. I cannot stress this point enough. I've hinted at this before, but now I'm going to say it rather bluntly. If your son is gay, that is *not* an excuse for you to shame him, disown him, or in any other way to disparage him. He is still your child, and he is a child of God. If you have to choose between your son and your religion, choose your son. Let your love for your son change your heart and motivate you to make changes in your church. Speak out against homophobia. Be a force for good. Even if the task seems insurmountable, you are planting a seed. It is also possible to love your religion and your son at the same time. Live with the conflict. Don't let the conflict ruin the relationship you have so carefully built with your son.

Baptism is extremely important to me. I see my children as gifts from God... and when I baptized them, I was thanking God for them and giving them back to God. In the Episcopal Church, we baptize infants. Children then have an opportunity when they are older, through Confirmation, to make an adult affirmation of the vows we made for them at their baptism. There are other faiths that dedicate infants and leave the baptism decision for each individual to decide for himself. Perhaps you are an atheist and don't believe in baptism at all. Do you believe in science? Teach your son to respect nature and the earth and all living things.

What gives you hope? Share that with your son. He will need it on the days that seem too difficult to bear. Is there some business philosophy that guides you? Personally, I value people and relationships. I believe when you take care of your people and build strong relationships, the money will take care of itself. I've really done my best to share that philosophy with both Tommy and Matt. Tommy and I have had many interesting discussions about this since he works for tips as a server. Make sure that your behavior is a living example of all the wisdom you have shared with your son. Be prepared for him to let you know when he sees you doing something that is not in line with the values that he knows are important to you. When he does, listen. Thank him for bringing it to your attention. Then, let him see how you go about making it right. No longer is it good enough to parent with the "Do as I say, not as I do" mentality. Nothing speaks more powerfully than being true to your word.

I have also prayed for myself as their mother, and for my children since they were conceived. One prayer I find particularly helpful and special is this:

—⋇—

"LORD, HELP ME RAISE MY CHILDREN TO KNOW, TO LOVE, AND TO SERVE YOU ALL THE DAYS OF THEIR LIVES."

In his book *The Prophet*, Kahlil Gibran said about children:

⌒⋇⌒

"Your children are not your children.

They are the sons and daughters of Life's longing for itself.

They come through you but not from you,

and though they are with you yet they belong not to you.

You may give them your love but not your thoughts,

for they have their own thoughts.

You may house their bodies but not their souls,

for their souls dwell in the house of tomorrow, which you cannot

visit, not even in your dreams.

You may strive to be like them, but seek not to make them like you.

for life goes not backward nor tarries with yesterday.

You are the bows from which your children as living arrows are sent forth.

The archer sees the mark upon the path of the infinite, and He bends

you with His might that His arrows may go swift and far.

Let your bending in the archer's hand be for gladness;

for even as He loves the arrow that flies,

so He loves also the bow that is stable."

The Prophet by Kahlil Gibran

Our children are with us for only a short time. Give your son your best, pray for him, love him, speak life over him, tell him the truth, teach him to tell the truth and to make good decisions for himself and then let him go. One day, you'll look up and see that the boy you worried about and fretted over has suddenly grown into a true gentleman... a reflection of the love and devotion which he could only have received from you. I believe that you will then look back on all those times you doubted yourself, and you will know with every fiber of your being that you are a wonderful mother!

I'm amazed that Matthew now talks to me about literally anything that is on his mind and heart. This is the same child who once refused to open up at all about his feelings, and especially not about dating or anything personal. Now, he tells his friends that I'm his best friend. One of my proudest moments in life was when Tommy once said to me, "Mom, you're perfect." I said, "No, I'm not." He replied, "You're the perfect mom for me!" My wish for you and your son is that you will experience that same joy, fulfillment, and loving relationship that I have found in my parenting journey with my sons.

TOMMY

I am so proud of my mom. She is the best mother I could've ever asked for, and it is amazing to see her chasing her dreams. Since the day I was born, my mom put everything that she had into raising me and my brother, Matthew. She always went the extra mile to ensure that her sons were not only taken care of but were thriving. She pushed both of us to find and pursue the things that we were passionate about -from me being in both band and theater to Matt playing football for basically his whole life. She has always been there for both of us when we needed her the most. Through the ups and downs, good and bad, she has always been there for me. When I finally came out to her at 18, even though she had already known for years, she fully supported me. She is truly an inspiration to me. I mean she is in her 50s and she's still reaching for the stars. Writing this book. Pursuing voiceover. Showing me that no matter how old you get, you should never be afraid to chase your dreams. I love this woman with all of my heart. I am so excited for all she has accomplished and all of the amazing things that are ahead of her, and I can't wait to support her through it just like she has always supported me.

MATT

Growing up with a mother like mine really helped me for the better. When I was younger, I didn't understand the "why" behind her decisions, but now that I'm older I understand her reasons. She taught me things by having conversations about our problems and conflicts. Growing up in my household made me an empathetic person and showed me how important communication is. Everyone is unique and understands things in different ways, so you have to learn to communicate in ways that people can understand. You also have to be able to assess yourself to see how you can become better. My mom taught me how to calm down and try to understand the person's feelings and emotions. In addition, she taught me how to deal with my own personal emotions and take ownership of my actions. She treated me like an adult, rather than looking down on me as some parents do with their children. I appreciate that she always took the time to hear what I had to say, even if she had to process and come back to it. When we had problems, she made sure to emphasize the lesson behind the conflict/situation, so we could learn to react better and maneuver after it was resolved. I began to develop a natural understanding of what's right and wrong which laid the foundation of my morals that I stand by. My mother's methods of raising us weren't the easiest but instead of ruling with an iron fist, my mother instilled empathy in us which helped us understand each other better and made our little family bond unbreakable.

ABOUT THE AUTHOR

I'm a divorced mom of two grown sons. I believe that everyone has worth and purpose in this life. I also believe that everyone is deserving of love. These two beliefs are the foundation of my parenting style. It sounds simplistic, but it has not been an easy road. There were many times when I doubted my choices, yet my heart would not allow me to parent any other way. Looking back, I'm so glad I stayed the course, trusting my instincts and doing what I knew was right, despite life's challenges.

My journey parenting two Black sons has included parenting through divorce, going back to work, childcare issues, my personal physical and mental health issues, having a child diagnosed on the autism spectrum, another child with a chronic health condition, dating, financial challenges, legal obstacles, and of course the fears of raising a Black son in today's social climate. A mother's job can feel overwhelming and isolating, but the rewards are great.

I'm also an audiobook narrator; voice actor; Reiki Master; and avid reader. I'm passionate about social issues affecting our sons, and I believe we must do everything within our power to set them up for success.